Super Predators
TIGERS

TJ Rob

Super-Predators: TIGERS
By TJ Rob

Copyright Text TJ Rob, 2017
All rights reserved. No part of the book may be reproduced in any form without permission in writing from the author. Reviewers may quote brief passages in review.

Disclaimer
No part of this book may be reproduced in any form or by any means, mechanical or electronic, including photocopying or recording, or by an information storage and retrieval system, or transmitted by email without permission in writing from the publisher. This book is for entertainment purposes only. The views expressed are those of author alone.

Published by:
TJ Rob
Suite 609
440-10816 Macleod Trail SE
Calgary, AB T2J 5N8   www.TJRob.com

ISBN 978-1-988695-50-1

Photo Credits: Images used under license from Flickr.com, Pixabay.com, Public Domain, Wikimedia Commons:

Cover page, Brian Mckay / Flickr.com; Back Page, Mathias Appel / Flickr.com; pg. 1, S. Taheri CC BY-SA 2.5 / Wikimedia Commons; pg. 2, BYus71 / Pixabay.com; pg. 3, BYus71 / Pixabay.com; pg. 4, Neil Turner / Flickr.com; pg. 5, Tambako the Jaguar / Flickr.com; pg. 6, Soren Wolf / Flickr.com ; pg. 7, Public Domain via Wikimedia Commons; pg. 9, Skeeze / Pixabay.com; pg. 9, OpenClipart-Vectors / Pixabay.com; pg. 10, Christine Majul / Flickr.com; pg. 10, Greverod CC-BY-SA-3.0 / Wikimedia Commons; pg. 11, Julie's hounds / Flickr.com; pg. 12, wildlifeartbykaz / Pixabay.com; pg. 13, Ali Arsh CC BY 2.0 / via Wikimedia Commons; pg. 13, Jack Fiallos / Flickr.com; pg. 14, Leo Messana / Flickr.com; pg. 14, Denise Chan / Flickr.com; pg. 15, Public Domain / Pixabay.com; pg. 16, Sundeep Kheria CC BY-SA 4.0 / via Wikimedia Commons; pg. 17, JP Bennett CC BY 2.0 / via Wikimedia Commons; pg. 17, Paul Asman and Jill Lenoble / Flickr.com; pg. 17, Dave Lonsdale / Flickr.com; pg. 17, JoeMurphy / Pixabay.com; pg. 17, mikepinkerton4x4 / Pixabay.com; pg. 18, Dan Gregson / Flickr.com; pg. 19, Tambako the Jaguar / Flickr.com; pg. 20, Public Domain / PublicDomainPictures.net; pg. 21, Tambako the Jaguar / Flickr.com; pg. 22, Tambako the Jaguar / Flickr.com; pg. 23, Pexels / Pixabay.com; pg. 24, Lauren Elyse Lynskey / Flickr.com; pg. 25, Shahbaz CC BY-SA 4.0 / via Wikimedia Commons; pg. 26, Chester Zoo / Flickr.com; pg. 27, Tambako the Jaguar / Flickr.com; pg. 28, Tambako the Jaguar / Flickr.com; pg. 29, Tambako the Jaguar / Flickr.com; pg. 30, Tambako the Jaguar / Flickr.com; pg. 31, Tambako the Jaguar / Flickr.com; pg. 32, Jean Francois Fournier / Flickr.com; pg. 33, Tambako the Jaguar / Flickr.com; pg. 34, Par Appaloosa CC BY-SA 3.0 / Wikimedia Commons; pg. 35, Par Appaloosa CC BY-SA 3.0 / Wikimedia Commons; pg. 36, Shane Gorski / Flickr.com; pg. 37, Tambako the Jaguar / Flickr.com; pg. 38, Pexels / Pixabay.com; pg. 39, Tambako the Jaguar / Flickr.com

TABLE OF CONTENTS

	Page
What are Tigers?	4
The origin of Tigers	5
How many types of Tigers are there?	6
Where do Wild Tigers live today?	7
Endangered Species	8
How big is a Tiger?	9
Tiger stripes	10
Why do Tigers have stripes?	11
Tiger fur	12
Tiger fur color	13
Tiger skin	15
Hunting	16
What do Tigers like to eat?	17
How do Tigers hunt?	18
Do Tigers roar?	20
Other sounds that Tigers make	21
How long do Tigers live?	22
7 Cool Tiger Facts	23
Giant Claws	24
Huge Teeth	26
Tiger Cubs	28
Do Tigers swim?	32
How much do Tigers sleep?	33
How have Tigers adapted to their environment?	34
Tiger territories	36
Tigers keep very clean	37
7 More Cool Tiger Facts	38
Threats to Tigers	39
Please leave a review / OTHER books by TJ Rob	40

What are Tigers?

Tigers are the largest of all the felines (the cat family) in the world. Throughout history, many cultures have considered the Tiger to be a symbol of strength and courage.

Tigers have extraordinary stripes which help camouflage them when hunting their prey. Some Tigers have orange fur with black stripes; others have tan stripes. Some have white fur with tan stripes and some very rare Tigers are all white.

Tigers are apex predators, which means that they have no predators that hunt them. They are at the top of the food chain.

The Origin of Tigers

The Tiger's closest living relatives were thought to be the Lion, Leopard and Jaguar. Genetic analysis has shown that the Tiger and the Snow Leopard are more closely related to each other than to the Lion, Leopard and Jaguar.

In the Gansu Province of North Western China, remains of an extinct Tiger relative called the Longdan Tiger, have been found. The fossils of this extinct Tiger were dated to over 2 Million years ago.

How many types are there?

All Tigers have the species name Panthera Tigris.

There were once 9 sub-species of Tigers.

Now only 6 sub-species of Tigers are left. 3 sub-species are extinct.

1	Bengal Tiger
2	Indo-Chinese Tiger
3	Malayan Tiger
4	Siberian Tiger
5	South Chinese Tiger
6	Sumatran Tiger

Where do Wild Tigers live today?

All Wild Tigers live in Asia. Although their numbers are few, Tigers live across 12 different countries.

The bigger Siberian Tiger lives in the Northern, colder areas, such as Eastern Russia and North Eastern China.

The other smaller Tiger subspecies live in Southern, warmer countries such as Bangladesh, Bhutan, Cambodia, India, Indonesia, Laos, Malaysia, Myanmar, Nepal and Vietnam.

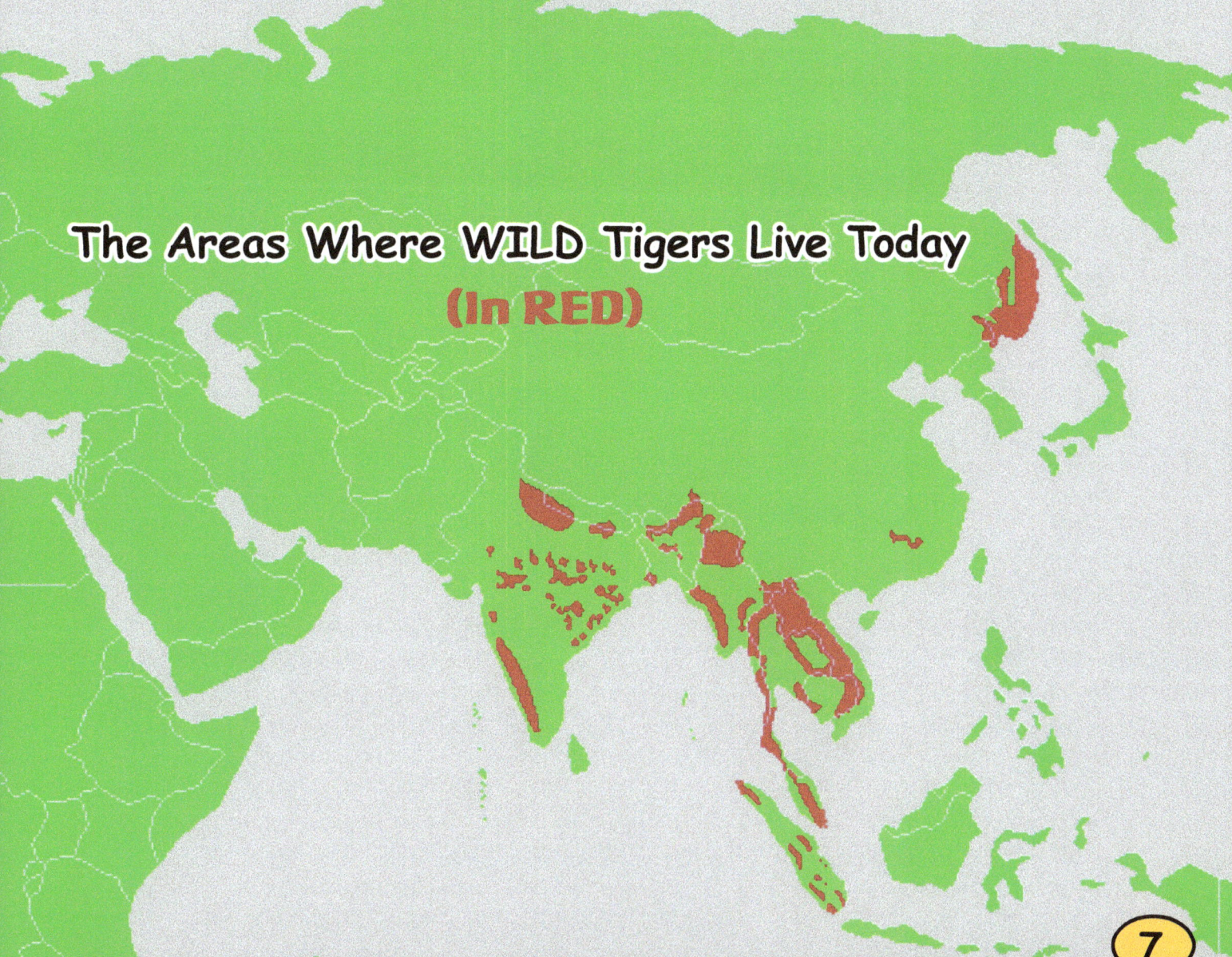

The Areas Where WILD Tigers Live Today (In RED)

ENDANGERED SPECIES

In the early 1900's, there were around 100,000 Wild Tigers throughout the world.

Today, only an estimated total of around 4,000 - 4,500 exist in the wild.

That is a huge drop of 95% from 120 years ago! Today ALL Tigers are endangered, facing extinction.

A breakdown of Tiger numbers by subspecies:

Bengal Tiger	Less than 2,000
Indo-Chinese Tiger	750 - 1300
Malayan Tiger	600 - 800
Sumatran Tiger	400 - 500
Siberian Tiger	About 450
South Chinese Tiger	Only 47 kept in zoos
Bali Tiger	EXTINCT
Caspian Tiger	EXTINCT
Javan Tiger	EXTINCT

How big is a Tiger?

Many people believe that Lions weigh more than Tigers.

Tigers are the ones which weigh more than Lions. Male Siberian Tigers weigh nearly 100 pounds (90 kg) more than male African Lions.

Females of all Tiger subspecies are smaller than the males.

The largest subspecies, the Siberian Tiger, can weigh up to 660 pounds (300 kg).

A 6 foot man VS an adult male Tiger

Tiger dimensions by the numbers

Height: 3 - 3.5 feet (.9 - 1.1 m) at the shoulders.

Length: Head and body length 4.6 - 9.2 feet (1.4 - 2.8 m) tail length 2 - 3 feet (.6 - .9 m).

Weight: 660 pounds (300 kg)

Tiger Stripes

Everyone recognizes the Tiger from its striped coat.

Most Tigers have between 100 - 150 stripes. Each Tiger subspecies has different patterns and numbers of stripes.

The Sumatran Tiger has the most stripes while the Siberian Tiger has the fewest. The Siberian Tiger's stripes are wider and lighter in color than those of the other subspecies.

No two Tigers have the same markings on their coats. They are as personal as fingerprints are for humans.

Every Tiger has it own number of stripes that vary in width and pattern. All Tigers have different numbers of stripes and different patterns from one side to the other.

2 Sumatran Tigers but different stripes

Why do Tigers have Stripes?

Tigers use their coats as camouflage.

Tiger stripes help them get as close to their prey as they can without being spotted. Their orange coloring helps them blend in with the grasses and ground cover, but without the stripes they would stick out like a big orange balloon!

The black stripes break up the orange color and make them harder to spot. Most animals in the wild do not see colors and dimensions as well as humans, so a solid object is much easier to see.

The black, white and gray of a Tiger's stripes may even look like shadows.

A Tiger blending into its surroundings

Tiger Fur

The thickness of a Tiger's fur depends on the area and climate in which the animal lives. In cooler, wetter climates, Tigers develop a thicker, longer coat. Underneath this longer fur is a soft layer of warm, fluffy fur. In hotter areas, the coat of the Tiger is much thinner and shorter.

Tigers have a white spot of fur on the back of each of their ears. These are called Ocelli. They look like another pair of "eyes", giving the impression that the Tiger can see in all directions at all times, even when it is facing the opposite direction.

Ocelli are also used in communication amongst Tigers. They swivel their ears around to show other Tigers these "eye" spots.

Ocelli behind each ear

Tiger Fur Color

Bengal Tigers are the only subspecies that come in different colors! Bengal Tigers have 4 different color variations.

Standard/Orange

The most common is the Orange and Black or Standard color.

White

Less common is the White (white with black stripes).

The Golden, Strawberry or Cinnamon (golden with reddish stripes) is extremely rare.

Golden/Strawberry/Cinnamon

White Tigers have a genetic defect that causes them to have white fur and blue eyes. White Tigers are not found in the wild, only in captivity. The white color is a result of unnatural inbreeding and cross-breeding.

Snow White

The most rare of all is the striking Snow White Bengal Tiger (white with faint gold stripes.)

In general, Northern Tigers (from Russia and Northern China) have lighter coats. Southern Tigers (from Malaysia and Sumatra) are darker.

Tiger Skin

Few people know that the skin of the Tiger underneath the patterned fur is also striped. The stripes go all the way through to the skin. So Tigers have striped skin, not just striped fur!

Zoo Veterinarians noticed this when they had to shave off sections of the fur coat to carry out surgery.

The darkness of the striped pattern in the skin depends on how dark the stripes are in the Tiger's fur.

The skin of the White Tiger is a bluish color, also complete with stripes.

Tiger Skin with Stripes

Hunting

Tigers mainly eat meat. On very rare occasions Tigers will eat fruits, berries and grasses (usually to aid digestion).

In order to survive, it is very important that Tigers become great hunters at a young age.

Stalking Tiger

Tigers are very good at moving quietly through the areas where their prey is found. Their stripes help to camouflage them so they will not be seen until it is too late.

Tigers look for the young, the weak, or the old in a group of animals. There is very little chance that these animals will be able to outrun them.

Tigers have to be very careful which animals they choose as their prey. Some of their prey are very dangerous and can injure or even kill them.

For example: Tigers often leave baby Elephants and Rhinos alone because of the physical strength of their parents.

What do Tigers like to eat?

Tigers mainly prey on large hoofed mammals, such as Wild Boar, Deer, Elk, Water Buffalo and Wild Cattle.

Depending on where they live, they even might kill and eat Leopards, Pythons, Crocodiles and Bears.

Sometimes they prey on domestic livestock raiding villages and farms for Cattle, Goats, Horses and Pigs.

Wild Boar

Nilgai Antelope

Sambar Deer

Gaur - Indian Bison

Manchurian Elk

Water Buffalo

How do Tigers Hunt?

Tigers normally hunt alone. There is no pack to support them.

On average Tigers hunt every 8 or 9 days. Tigers rely mainly on their sight and hearing rather than their sense of smell. Tigers do most of their hunting at night. They can also hunt during the day if they are really hungry.

Tigers usually stalk and ambush their prey. At night, their stripes help them hide in thick underbrush, trees and grass as they slowly creep toward their prey.

When they are close enough - 20 to 30 feet (6 to 9 meters) - they break from hiding, race toward their unsuspecting prey and then attack. Tigers are able to reach a speed of up to 50 miles (80 km), per hour. This speed is used for very short distances only - to make the final attack on their prey. Tigers cannot run for long distances.

To kill large animals, Tigers bite their throats. To kill animals smaller than half their size, they clamp down on the back of the neck.

The Tiger will then drag the kill to a sheltered spot in which it can eat in peace. A Tiger can eat up to 88 pounds (40 Kg) of meat in one night.

What it does not finish, it will hide away, returning to eat these leftovers later or the following day.

Even though they are great hunters, Tigers are only successful in 1 out of 20 attempted kills.

Do Tigers Roar?

Yes they do roar.

Why do Tigers roar?

Tigers generally only roar at other Tigers. When they roar they communicate with other Tigers in their group or they let other Tigers know where their territory is.

Tigers do not roar before attacking another species of animal.

A Tiger's roar can be heard as far as 2 miles (3.3 km) away.

Other sounds that Tigers make

What other sounds do Tigers make?

Tigers, Snow Leopards and Clouded Leopards make a sound called "chuffing" by rumbling their throat and blowing air through their nostrils. It is similar to the sound we make when we clear our throat.

Chuffing is used between Tigers who are greeting each other, during courting, or simply by a mother comforting her cubs.

Do Tigers purr?

Unlike some of the big cats like Cougars, Tigers do not purr because muscle development in their larynx (the voice box) is weak.

Generally, if a cat can roar they cannot purr, and if they can purr they cannot roar.

How long do Tigers live?

In the wild, on average Tigers live 8 to 10 years. Some may live even longer - for 15 or 20 years.

In captivity, they live as long as 26 years.

7 Cool Tiger Facts:

1. The Tiger is the biggest species of the Cat family.

2. A group of Tigers is known as an 'ambush' or 'streak'.

3. There are more Tigers held in captivity than than there are in the Wild.

4. Your Cat at home shares 95.6% of its DNA with Tigers.

5. There are no Wild Tigers in Africa. Only in Asia.

6. All Cats, from Lions and Tigers right down to Domestic Cats, cannot taste anything sweet.

7. The Bengal Tiger is the national animal of India.

GIANT Claws

The claws of a Tiger can reach an amazing 5 inches (or almost 13 cm) in length. That is roughly the length of a cell phone! Claws are retractable and do not cause discomfort when they are not being used.

The 2 forefeet (front feet) have 5 claws in total. There are 4 regular claws and 1 specialized claw called a dewclaw. The dewclaw is located farther back on the foot and does not touch the ground when walking.

The hind (back) feet have 4 claws, but no dewclaw.

Giant Claws for scratching

How do Tigers use their claws?

- **As lethal weapons during the hunt.** The hook shape of each claw helps the Tiger to grab onto the skin of its prey and prevent its escape.

- **For cleaning.** Besides licking themselves to stay clean, Tigers often use their claws to scratch themselves. This dislodges dead hair, deals with skin irritations and removes tangles in their fur.

- **To mark out territory by scratching trees.** Once a tree is chosen the Tiger uses it over and over again. It leaves deep scratch marks on the trunk of the tree. Not all Tigers scratch trees - some do it often while others don't scratch trees at all. The height of the claw marks on a tree can indicate the Tiger's size.

- **For tree climbing.** Tigers seldom climb trees, but they can when they need to. They may do this if being chased by dogs or when they are chasing their prey. Tiger claws help make climbing upwards more easy. Climbing down is more difficult. The angle of the Tiger's claws are not able to help it grip onto the tree on the way down.

- **For defense.** Mainly against other Tigers, but also with other animals and when a cat feels threatened by man.

Claws for tree climbing

HUGE Teeth

Tigers have the longest teeth of any of the Cat family. Some large Tigers have teeth measuring 4 inches (10 cm) long. That is about the size of a man's middle finger. A canine tooth of a Tiger is larger and longer than that of a similar-sized Lion.

Tigers have have 30 teeth, which are designed to help them to grip struggling prey, break bones and rip flesh.

Their jaws are also very powerful. They are made for snapping the necks of their prey, crunching through bone and sinew and grinding meat into mouthfuls soft enough to swallow.

Their canine teeth are very sharp. These canine teeth have pressure-sensing nerves so the Tiger knows exactly where to deliver the killing bite to its prey. If a Tiger lost its canines, it would not be able to kill prey and eat.

4 Huge Canine Teeth

Cubs are born with a set of milk teeth which are slowly replaced by adult teeth. This process starts when the Tiger is about 6 months of age.

The baby teeth are not pushed out in the same way as with humans. The adult set forms beside the milk teeth. Once the adult teeth are well grown in, the milk teeth will fall out. This prevents an animal that needs its teeth for killing and eating its prey from ever having gaps in its mouth.

A bite from an adult Tiger's jaws can generate pressure of up to 10,000 pounds per square inch. That is enough pressure to crunch through the vertebrae of any creature on the earth!

Tiger Cubs

4 month-old Siberian cubs playing

Tiger babies are called cubs.

Most of the time adult Tigers live on their own, except when they wish to mate with each other. After mating they go their own way.

The females give birth approximately 16 weeks after mating. Tiger cubs are born blind and are completely dependent on their mother. Newborn Tiger cubs weigh between 1.75 to 3.5 pounds (.785 to 1,6 kg).

Females rear their cubs in dens in places like thickets and rocky crevices. Tiger mothers protect and guard their cubs from wandering males that may kill the cubs.

A female may have a litter of 3 to 4 cubs at a time, every 2 years. Only about half of all cubs survive their first two years. If all the cubs in 1 litter die, a second litter may be produced within 5 months.

Tiger mother sorting out her cubs

Siberian Tiger cub exploring

29

A Tiger cub's eyes will open between 6 to 12 days after birth. However, cubs do not have full vision for a few weeks. Tiger cubs are born with blue eyes which turn to yellow when they become older. Only White Tigers keep their blue eyes into adulthood.

The mother will feed her cubs milk from her body for about 8 weeks before they go out of the den with her.

Tigers are mostly independent at 2 years of age. Cubs leave their mothers at about 2 to 3 years.

Tigers become fully grown at 3 to 4 years of age. Females are able to have their own cubs at age 3 to 4, and Males at age 4 to 5 years.

Very young Tiger cubs have blue eyes

Tiger mother licking her cub

Do Tigers swim?

Tigers usually live in tropical jungle environments, where there is a lot of water.

Tigers are excellent swimmers and during the day are often found relaxing in ponds, streams, and rivers. They look for water to cool off in during hot days. Tigers are one of the few Cats that like swimming and love spending time in the water.

Tigers are such strong swimmers that they can even tread through water while carrying their prey.

Tigers have been known to swim across rivers that are 4.3 miles (7 km) Wide. They have been seen swimming up to 18 miles (29 km) in a single day.

Tigers love water

How much do Tigers sleep?

A sleeping Tiger

Tigers are just like domestic house cats that spend a lot of time resting or sleeping. A Tiger will spend between 16 and 20 hours each day just lying in the shade.

Tigers from tropical climates frequently choose to rest in shallow water holes.

Tigers hunt mostly at night. Between the hours of 8 a.m. and 4 p.m. they generally spend their time resting and sleeping.

How have Tigers adapted to their environment?

Great vision to easily see prey

Razor sharp Canines and powerful jaws to kill prey

Long retractable Claws to grab prey and to mark territory

Flexible spine to help with leaping onto prey

Black stripes for camouflage

Long back legs help with jumping

A long tail helps with balance

Loose skin around the stomach helps avoid being hurt if kicked

Tiger Territories

Tigers fiercely guard the territories where they live and roam. They mark their territories and have been known to fight one another for territory.

A Tiger's Territory is where adult Tigers live. This area is able to satisfy all of the Tiger's needs. Tigers normally limit their movements to within their territory. Female Tigers or Tigresses use their territory to give birth to their cubs and raise them.

Within their territory, a Tiger may have a number of dens in caves, hollow trees, and dense vegetation. They can easily protect themselves by hiding from danger in one of these dens. A Tigress needs about 5.5 square miles (20 square km). A male Tiger needs a larger territory to roam around in, of about 23 to 30 square miles (60 to 100 square km).

Most Tigers have territories that are close to water, such as a lake, pond or river, to cool off and drink. They can travel 6 to 12 miles (10 to 19 km) in 1 night as they check out the boundaries of their territory.

Tigers keep very clean

Tigers are very clean animals.

Tigresses never take meat into their dens to feed their cubs.

Food is eaten outside of the den.

They constantly lick their cubs to keep them clean.

Tigers are different from hoofed animals like Cattle, Buffalo and Deer. Tigers very rarely poop or urinate in the water they use for drinking or bathing. Big cats are very fussy regarding their toilet. Both in captivity and in the wild, Tigers will move a distance away from their sleeping quarters, and where they eat.

The Tiger's tongue plays a very important part in hygiene and cleanliness. A Tiger will lick its paws and use them to wipe over its face, ears and forehead. This is identical to how a domestic Cat keeps itself clean.

A Tiger's tongue produces antiseptic saliva. Any injuries are carefully licked and coated with this special antiseptic saliva. This helps to prevent a wound from becoming infected.

7 MORE Cool Tiger Facts:

1. Tigers have the 2nd largest brain of all carnivores, the largest being the brain of the Polar bear.

2. Tigers have eyes with round pupils, unlike domestic Cats, which have pupils with slits.

3. Tigers cannot purr. To show happiness, Tigers squint or close their eyes. When they squint or close their eyes, they lower their defenses. Tigers will only do this when they feel comfortable and safe.

4. A Tiger has color vision just like humans. A Tiger's night vision is 6 times better than that of humans.

5. Tigers that breed with Lions give birth to hybrids known as "Tigons" and "Ligers." This only happens in captivity as Lions and Tigers in the wild live in different parts of the world.

6. Tiger urine smells like buttered popcorn.

7. A Tiger's hearing is nearly five times better than ours.

THREATS TO TIGERS

Climate Change:

Tigers are feeling the effects of climate change as the planet warms. As sea levels rise and sea water moves up river, naturally fresh water is becoming much more salty. This forces Tigers to move towards areas populated with humans - the chances of animal/human conflicts is much higher than before.

Poaching:

Tigers are illegally killed or poached because their pelts are valuable in the black market trade and their body parts are used in traditional Asian medicines.

Human Populations are growing bigger:

Tigers are forced to compete for space with dense and often growing human populations. Human encroachment into Tiger habitat areas also decreases prey animals that Tigers can hunt.

THANKS FOR READING!

Please leave a review at the website where you bought this book and tell others what you liked about it.

Visit www.TJRob.com to get a FREE eBook and to learn about other exciting books by TJ Rob:

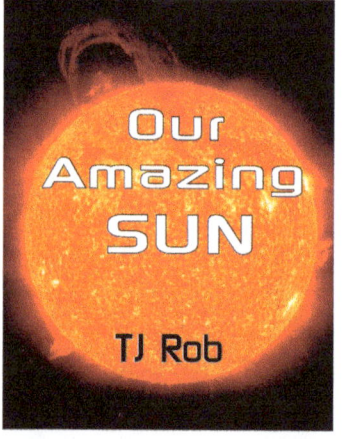

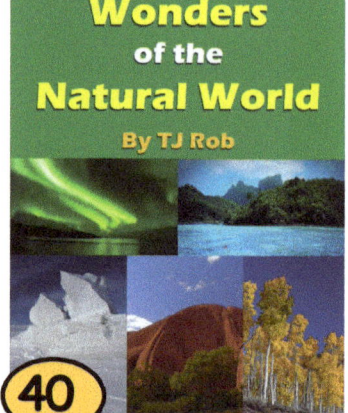
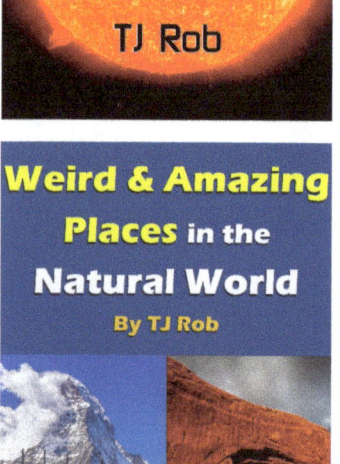
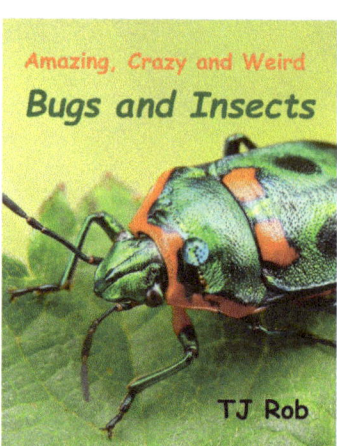
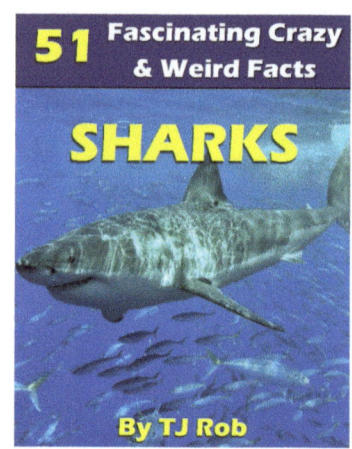

www.ingramcontent.com/pod-product-compliance
Lightning Source LLC
Chambersburg PA
CBHW040005080526
44586CB00027B/2890